Super-Duper Science

Snips & Snails

by Annalisa McMorrow
illustrated by Marilynn G. Barr

Publisher: Roberta Suid
Design & Production: Scott McMorrow
Educational Consultant: Shirley Ross
Cover Design: David Hale
Cover Art: Mike Artell

Also in this series: *Ladybug, Ladybug* (MM 2015), *Twinkle, Twinkle* (MM 2016), *Rub-a-Dub-Dub* (MM 2017), *Pussycat, Pussycat* (MM 2036), *Daffy-Down-Dilly* (MM 2037), *Rain, Rain, Go Away!* (MM 2038), *Sticks and Stones* (MM 2097), *Wheels on the Bus* (MM 2098), and *A Diller, A Dollar* (MM 2099)

CONTENTS

INTRODUCTION

Snips & Snails is composed of five chapters, each a complete unit dedicated to a specific type of creature. This resource has a cross-curricular approach that helps children develop a hands-on understanding of science while strengthening language skills, such as speaking and listening. Children will relate to the natural world in a personal way: learning through games, observations, movements, songs, literature links, and art.

Let's Read features a popular children's book, such as *Lyle, Lyle Crocodile* by Bernard Waber, and is accompanied by a detailed plot description. **Let's Talk** helps children link the featured book with familiar feelings, thoughts, or ideas in their own lives. For example, in the Snakes chapter, the "Let's Talk" discussion focuses on a time when something in the children's life was changing. This page also includes a pattern that can be duplicated and used as a bookmark.

Let's Learn is filled with facts about each creature. For example, some people think snakes are slimy, but they're not. Choose facts that you think will interest the children. Read a fact a day during the unit. Or write different facts down and post them on bulletin boards around the room.

The **Let's Create** activities in each chapter allow children to use their imaginations while acquiring small motor skills. The children will make their own sock snakes and margarine tub turtles, create chameleon stick puppets, make hidden chameleon pictures, and much more.

Children make a hands-on learning connection in the **Let's Find Out** activities. These projects focus on exploration, leading children through moments of discovery as they find out about chameleon tongues, learn what it's like to move like a snake, discover how lizards shed, and much more.

Let's Play suggests a new game to interest children in the creature of the moment. **Let's Eat** offers suggestions for snacks that tie into the chapter's theme. A song sung to a familiar tune is featured in the **Let's Sing** section. Children can learn the new lyrics and perform them for parents or each other. Duplicate the songs and send them home with the children to share with their families.

Informative Pattern Pages complete each chapter. These patterns can be duplicated and used for bulletin board displays, reduced for cubby labels or name tags, or used for desk labeling. (Children can color the patterns using crayons or markers.)

At the end of the book, you'll find a Storybook Resources section filled with additional fiction picture books and storybooks, plus a Nonfiction Resources section listing factual and photographic books.

All About Snakes, Slugs, Snails...and More

Most of the animals featured in this book are reptiles. Reptiles have lived on the earth for more than 300 million years. They were around even before the dinosaurs! All reptiles are cold-blooded. This means that their bodies stay the same temperature as the air around them. Human beings (and all other mammals) are warm-blooded. Mammals stay the same body temperature regardless of the temperature outside. Reptiles have backbones and scaly skins. Despite what many people think, reptiles are smooth, not slimy, to the touch.

Reptiles include tortoises and turtles, crocodiles and alligators, and snakes and lizards.

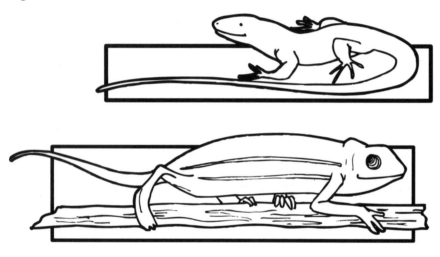

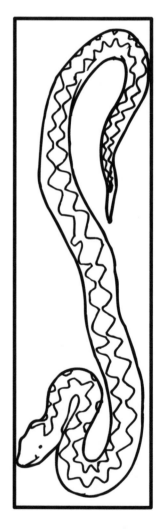

Snails and slugs are not reptiles, and they *are* sort of slimy. These creatures belong to a group of animals called mollusks. Other mollusks include clams, octopuses, and squid.

During these units, consider taking the children to a zoo, wildlife park, or aquarium to see some of the animals they're studying. However, remind the children that most wild animals prefer to live in the outdoors rather than as pets. For example, chameleons, which are transported from Africa, often die on the journey or soon after.

Snakes

Introduction

• Let's Read:
Verdi by Jannel Cannon (Harcourt Brace, 1997).
Verdi is a small yellow python who loves being yellow with black spots. He doesn't want to shed his skin and turn into a large, green sleepy python. He has too much energy! He likes to leap and do figure eights in the sky. When Verdi grows up, others expect him to settle down. Instead, he teaches the young yellow pythons all his old tricks.

• Let's Talk:
Verdi doesn't want to grow up. However, when he does get bigger, he finds that he can still do some of the things he did when he was younger. Plus he can teach other young snakes how to do them. Ask the children to share times when something in their lives was changing, and then discuss whether the event turned out to be positive or negative. Some examples might be having a new sibling, moving to a new house, starting a new school, or going on a trip.

• Let's Learn:
Snakes belong to a group of animals called reptiles. They have long bodies and no legs. Snakes' eyes are open all the time! They don't have eyelids. They can't chew their food, so they swallow it whole. Snakes have a long backbone and many ribs. Snakes don't have outer ears. They hear by "feeling" vibrations in the ground. Although some people think that snakes are wet or slimy, their skin is actually dry and cool. There are about 2,500 types of snakes. Only about 50 are harmful to humans.

Refer to the **Nonfiction Resources** at the end of the book for a list of resources that feature color pictures of snakes.

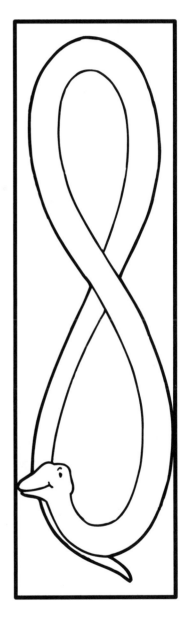

Snakes

Let's Create: Little Verdis

The children can make playdough snakes that look like the young Verdi. Tell the children that snakes come in all sorts of sizes. They can be as short as a child's finger or as long as a city bus!

What You Need:
Yellow and black playdough

What You Do:
1. Give each child a small ball of yellow playdough.
2. Show the children how to roll out the playdough to make a snake shape.
3. Let the children add black playdough spots to their snakes.
4. The children can make as many different lengths of snakes as they want. They can coil the snakes into figure eights, in honor of Verdi.

Options:
• Provide a variety of colors of playdough for the children to make different colored snakes. Tell the children that there are more than 2,500 different kinds of snakes in the world. Show pictures of different snakes for children to copy, or let them make up their own colorful snakes.

• Give children plastic eggs (available around Easter). They can coil their snakes and store them in the eggs. Explain that most snakes hatch from eggs.

Snakes

Let's Create: Super Sock Puppets

What You Need:
Socks (one per child), colored felt (red and other colors), glue

What You Do:
1. Cut out circles from the felt. Make two per child. (These will be the eyes.)
2. Cut out red forked tongues for the puppets. Make one per child.
3. Have the children put the socks on their hands.
4. Describe the importance of a snake's tongue. The snake's tongue helps it to "smell." (The tongue brings the smells back to a special organ in the snake's mouth.) Have each child glue on the eyes and tongues.
5. Let the children decorate the puppets with bits of felt.
6. The children can act out the story of *Verdi* as you read it. Or let the children put on puppet shows of their own.

Options:
• Provide wiggly eyes for the puppets.
• Bring in green socks and yellow socks for children to use to dramatize Verdi's different stages.
• Bring in knee-length nylons. Let the children cover their puppets with the nylons. They can then remove the nylons to demonstrate how snakes shed.

Snakes

Let's Create: "Snake, Rattle, and Roll" Rattles

A type of snake, called a rattlesnake, has a rattle at the end of its tail. When the snake wants to frighten its enemies, it shakes the rattle very fast.

What You Need:
Small plastic juice containers (with lids), coarse sand or fine gravel, packing tape, taped music, tape recorder

What You Do:
1. Describe rattlesnakes to the children.
2. Explain that they will be making their own rattles.
3. Give each child a plastic juice container.
4. Have the children fill their containers about one-third of the way with the sand or gravel.
5. Put a lid on each container and seal with packing tape.
6. Let the children shake their rattles to taped music. They can pretend to be rattlesnakes saying, "Watch out!"

Option:
• Provide glue and paper scraps for the children to use to decorate their rattles.

Snakes

Let's Create: Slithering Snake Jewelry

What You Need:
Aluminum foil, black and red construction paper, scissors

What You Do:
1. Explain that for thousands of years, snakes have appeared in art. They have been used on pottery and in jewelry. Bracelets and armbands that resemble snakes have been fashionable throughout history.
2. Give each child a section of aluminum foil.
3. Demonstrate how to roll the foil to create a snake-shape.
4. The children can cut out black eyes and red tongues from construction paper to glue onto their snakes.
5. Once the glue dries, the children can coil their snakes to wear as armbands or bracelets.
6. Let the children take home their snake jewelry.

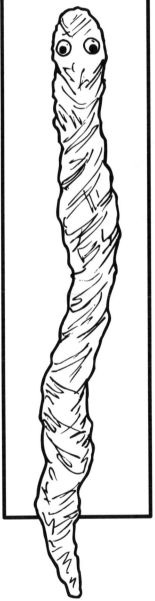

Snakes

Let's Find Out: How Snakes Move

Snakes don't have legs or feet. So how do they move around? They slither along the ground on their bellies!

What You Need:

A clean floor space, preferably covered with mats (such as tumbling mats)

What You Do:

1. Explain to the children that snakes don't have legs or feet. Ask the children to guess how snakes move around.
2. Discuss the ground rules: no touching; stop when the signal is given. Then let the children slide or slither across the floor, trying to move without using their hands or feet.
3. Stop the children and call on one child at a time to show the others his or her "snake moves." Point out snake-like characteristics.
4. Then let all of the children slither around some more.

Option:

• Different snakes move in different ways. Fat snakes creep in an almost straight line. Sometimes snakes wriggle by pushing against rocks or other hard objects. Their bodies seem to move in waves. Have the children practice moving in different ways.

Snakes

Let's Find Out: Long Snakes

The longest python ever found was 33 feet (11 m). It lived in the jungles of Thailand.

What You Need:
Tape measure, chalk

What You Do:
1. Describe the longest python.
2. Explain that the children will be working together to find out how many children it takes to be as long as a python.
3. Help the children measure a distance of 33 feet (11 m). Use a piece of chalk to mark the start and the end of the distance.
4. Have the children join in a straight line between the two marks. Keep adding children until they reach the end of the mark. If there aren't enough children to reach between the two marks, invite children from another class to help out. Or use X's to keep track of the children from the start of the line, and let them go to the end of the line to help out.
5. Count the children to find out how many children equal the length of the python.

Options:
• Let the children use the tape measure to find the length of objects in the classroom. Do simple math with them to figure out how many desks, tables, or other objects it takes to be as long as the python.
• Let the children line up books, erasers, chairs, or blocks end to end to measure the python's length.

Snakes

Let's Find Out: How Snakes Hide
In the hot desert, snakes bury under the sand to protect themselves from the sun.

What You Need:
Hiding Snakes (p. 15), sand table, sandbox, or aluminum baking pans, sticks or other "drawing" tools

What You Do:
1. Show the children the pictures that depict how snakes hide in the sand. Explain that the snake's movements bring sand over its back. The snake's scales help to move the sand evenly along its body.
2. When the snake is under the sand, all that's visible is its head and the marks behind it in the sand.
3. Point out in the picture that the snake leaves S-shaped marks in the sand.
4. Let the children take turns drawing S shapes at the sand table, in the aluminum pans, or in the sandbox. They can pretend a desert snake has just buried itself beneath the sand to avoid the heat.

Options:
• Have the children practice writing other letters in the sand. Lead them through the alphabet!
• Use this time to discuss how people should protect themselves from the heat. Remind children to wear hats and sunglasses on sunny days and have plenty of sunscreen available.

Hiding Snakes

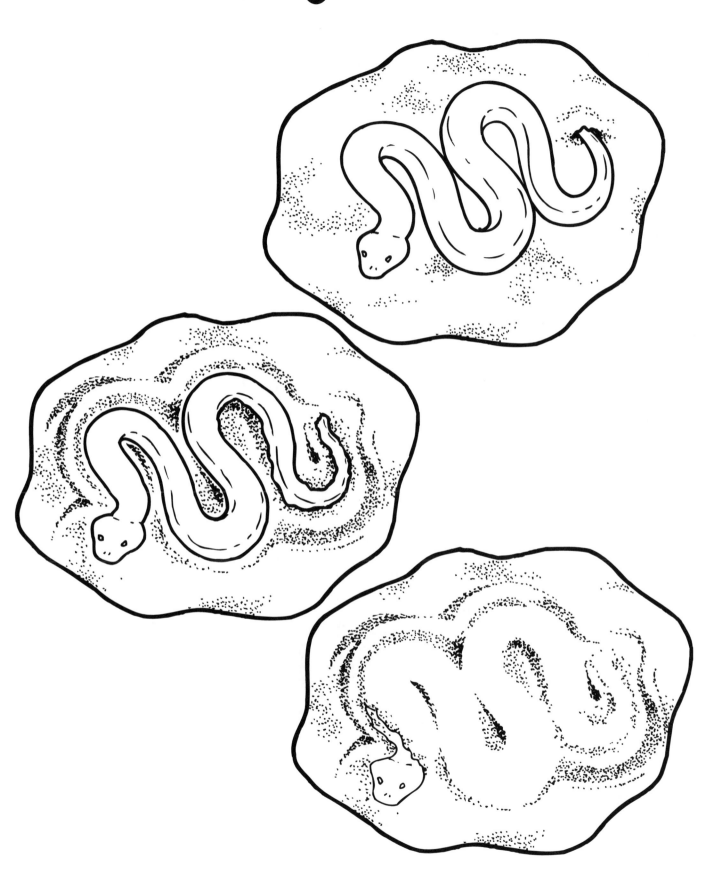

Snakes

Let's Play: Snake Tag

What You Need:
Nothing

What You Do:
1. Choose one child to be the leader of the snake.
2. The rest of the children are "free agents." They try to run away from the leader, who tries to tag them.
3. When a child is tagged, he or she joins onto the snake leader by placing one hand on the leader's shoulder. The other hand can be used to try to tag other children.
4. As more children are tagged, they join the chain, always keeping one hand on the shoulder of the child in front.
5. The last child tagged can be the lead snake in the next round.

Let's Play: Silent Snake Squeeze
Some snakes are very strong. They squeeze their dinner before eating it. Children can practice their silent snake squeezes with this game.

What You Need:
Nothing

What You Do:
1. Have the children sit in a circle holding hands.
2. Explain that you are going to pass a rhythm around the circle. You will squeeze the hand of the child next to you. That child will then pass the same sequence of squeezes onto the child next to him or her. The rhythm sequence will pass around the entire circle. Once it does, let another child start the squeeze sequence.

Snakes

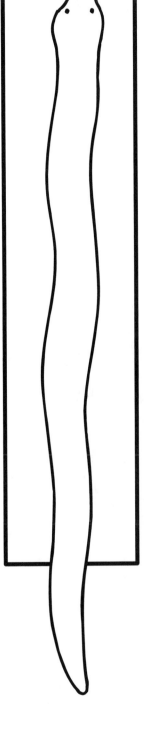

Let's Play: Sorting Snakes

What You Need:
Snake Patterns (p. 18), construction paper (in a variety of colors), scissors, basket

What You Do:
1. Duplicate the snakes onto different colors of construction paper and cut them out. Make many snakes.
2. Gather all the snakes together on the floor.
3. Have the children work together to sort the snakes. They can first sort them by color. Then they can mix the snakes up again and sort them by size.
4. The children can do this activity in groups or on their own. Store the snakes in a basket for later sorting.

Option:
• Use different colors of thick yarn for the snakes. Cut them in three or four different lengths. Use the snakes to create linear patterns. For example, children can use the snakes to make patterns of short, short, long, or short, long, long, short, and so on.

Snake Patterns

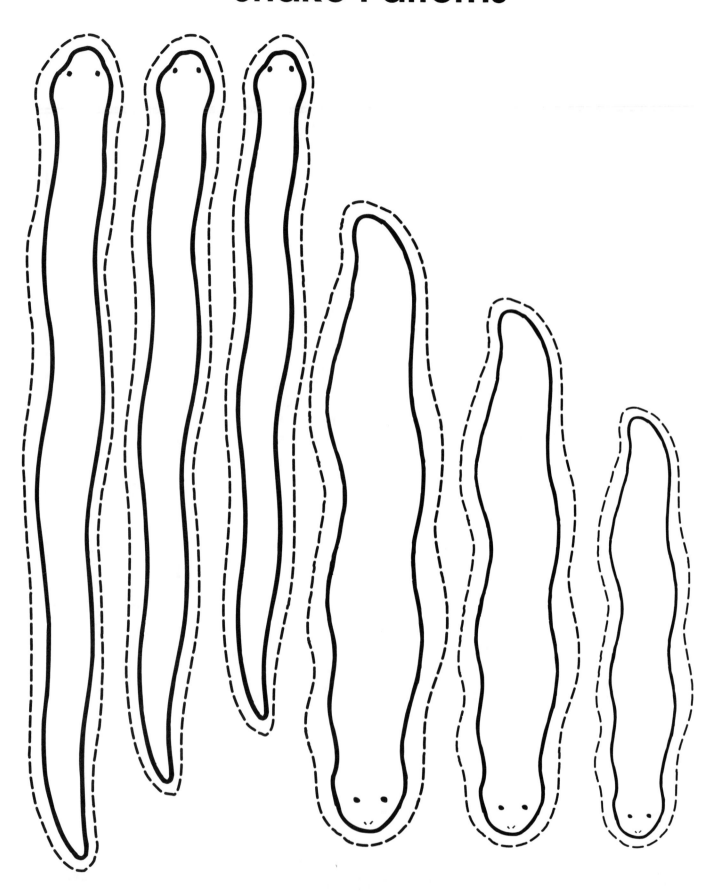

Snakes

Let's Eat: Scrumptious Snake Snacks

Different snakes eat different things. Flying snakes eat lizards, birds, frogs, and bats. Some snakes eat mice. Big snakes, like the python, eat goats and pigs. One type of snake eats only birds' eggs!

What You Need:
Chopped hard-boiled eggs, mayonnaise, crackers, salt and pepper, large bowl and spoon

What You Do:
1. Prepare a simple egg salad by mixing the chopped eggs and mayonnaise and seasoning to taste with salt and pepper.
2. Serve a small amount to each child.
3. Children can eat their egg salad with crackers while pretending to be snakes.

Let's Eat: Spaghetti Snake Snack

Instead of eating food that snakes eat, children will eat food that looks like snakes!

What You Need:
Spaghetti, grated cheese

What You Do:
1. Boil and drain the spaghetti away from the children.
2. Serve the spaghetti hot and let the children sprinkle on grated cheese.
3. Let the children slurp up their snake-shaped snack!

Snakes

Let's Sing: I'm a Little Egg Snake
(to the tune of "I'm a Little Teapot")

I'm a little egg snake,
I eat eggs.
I don't have feet, arms, or legs.
When I want to move from here to there,
I just slither without a care.

Let's Sing: Rattlesnake Rock
(to the tune of "Jingle Bell Rock")

Rattlesnake, rattlesnake, rattlesnake rock.
Rattlesnake glide and rattlesnake slide.
Rattle your rattler, and rattle it right,
Every day and night.

Rattlesnake, rattlesnake, rattlesnake rock.
Rattlesnake shimmy, rattlesnake shake.
Rattle your rattler, and rattle it right.
Every day and night!

Note: Let children shake their "Snake, Rattle, and Roll"
rattles (p. 10) to this song!

Option:
• Play a recording of "I'm Being Eaten by a Boa Constrictor"
(by Shel Silverstein) for the children.

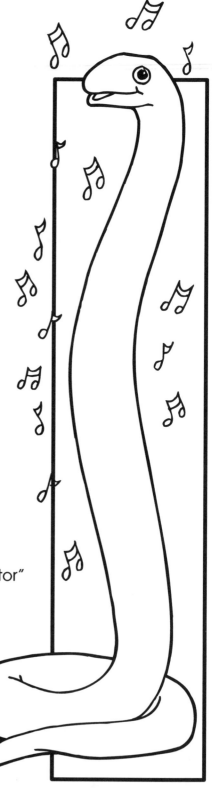

"I'm a Snake!"

Lizards

Introduction

• Let's Read:

A color of his own by Leo Lionni (Pantheon, 1975).
All animals have their own colors, except chameleons.
Chameleons change color to blend with their
surroundings. One little chameleon wishes he could have
a color of his own. He tries to stay the same color, but his
plans don't work. Finally, he meets another chameleon.
Although they still don't have their own color, they change
colors together.

• Let's Talk

Discuss the fact that the little chameleon is sad until he
finds a friend. Have the children share times when they did
things with friends and times when they did things on their
own. They can talk about whether they preferred being
with friends or being alone. Point out that either answer is
fine and that most people enjoy spending some time
alone and some time with friends.

• Let's Find Out

Chameleons, like the one in Leo Lionni's book, are a type
of animal called a reptile and a type of reptile called a
lizard. Most lizards have five toes on their feet, eyelids, and
ears visible on their heads. (This makes them very different
from snakes, which are also reptiles.) Chameleons are
found in Africa, Asia, and Europe. Chameleons have a
poor sense of smell. They are also almost deaf. However,
they have incredible vision. They notice all movements
around them. There are 100 different species of
chameleon!

Refer to the **Nonfiction Resources** at the end of the book
for a list of resources that feature color pictures of lizards.

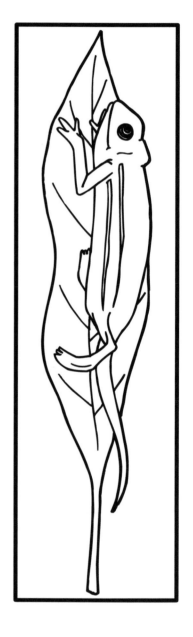

Lizards

Let's Create: Chameleon Puppets

What You Need:
Lizard Stencils (p. 24), colored paper (yellow, purple, green, red, black), heavy paper, scissors, Popsicle sticks, glue, crayons

What You Do:
1. Duplicate the Lizard Stencils onto heavy paper and cut out. Make enough for each child to have one.
2. Have the children trace the Lizard Stencils onto colored paper. Each child can make one lizard of each color.
3. Help the children cut out the lizards.
4. Demonstrate how to glue a Popsicle stick to the back of each lizard.
5. Once the glue has dried, read the story *A color of his own*. As you read the story, have the children hold up the correctly colored chameleons. They can call out the name of the color as they hold up their chameleon puppets.

Options:
• Have the children each make one puppet that is tiger striped and one that is red with white polka dots. Then they will have a complete set to go with the story.
• Provide wiggly eyes for the children to glue to their puppets.
• Send the chameleon puppets home with the children. They can practice the color names with their families.

Lizard Stencils

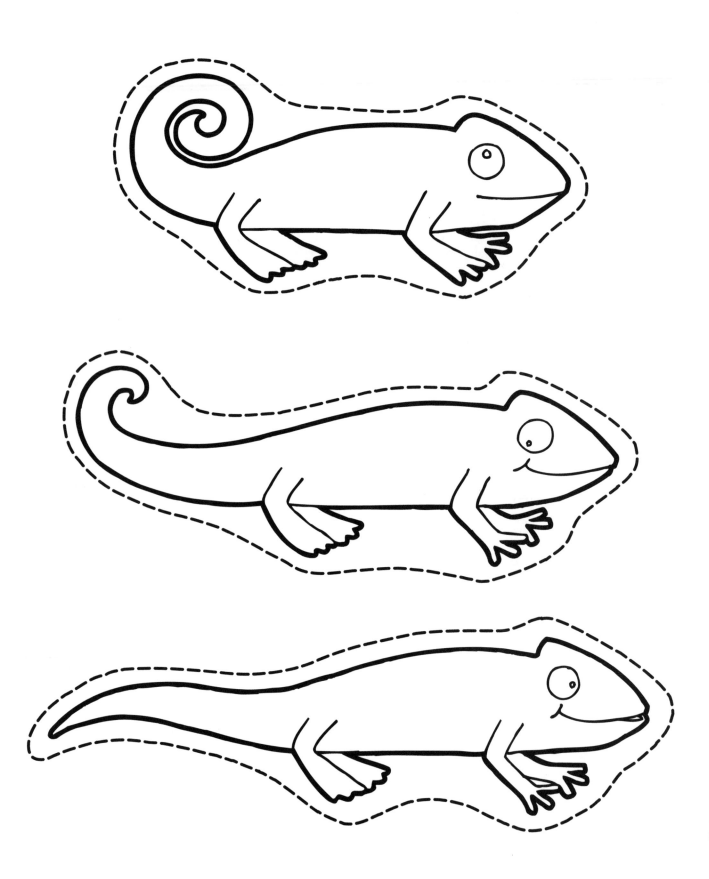

Lizards

Let's Create: Hidden Chameleon Pictures

Chameleons have a skin that changes pattern and color. This helps them blend in with their surroundings and hide from their enemies. Blending also helps them to catch their food. The insects don't see the chameleons, so the chameleons can catch them.

What You Need:
Lizard Stencils (p. 24), watercolors, paper, paintbrushes, scissors

What You Do:
1. Cut out enough lizards for each child to have one.
2. Give each child a sheet of paper.
3. Have the children use the watercolors to paint pictures.
4. Once the papers dry, give each child a lizard stencil.
5. The children can trace the lizards onto their papers. They can trace as many lizards as they want.
6. Provide black crayons or markers for the children to use to add features to the lizards.
7. Post the pictures on a "We're Hiding" bulletin board. Have visitors to the classroom spot the lizards in the pictures.

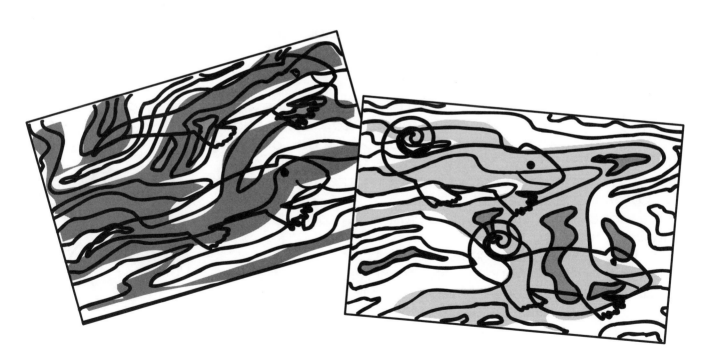

Lizards

Let's Create: Goldilocks and the Three Iguanas

Iguanas are lizards that live in the desert, the rain forest, and by the ocean. They have been on the earth for thousands of years! The word iguana (ee-GWAH-nuh) is a Spanish word. It means a large type of lizard.

What You Need:
Goldilocks and the Three Iguanas puppets (p. 27), crayons and markers, scissors

What You Do:
1. Duplicate a copy of the puppets for each child. Help children cut out their puppets.
2. Let the children color their puppets.
3. Discuss the concepts of small, medium, and large. Have the children pay attention each time you mention the different sizes of objects or characters in the story.
4. Tell the story of Goldilocks, using the word "iguanas" instead of "bears." (The children can use their puppets to act out the story as you tell it.)
5. After you finish the story, take a walk. Have the children look for objects that come in different sizes, such as cars, flowers, trees, and buildings. Or have the children look for various sizes of objects in the room, such as blocks, books, and dolls.

Note:
Consider setting the story in a desert or rain forest, since these are two places where iguanas are found. Also, consider adding other iguana facts to the story. For example, instead of having the iguanas go for a walk, they might be basking in the sun. Because iguanas are tree dwelling, their house might be a tree house. Other iguana facts to use:
• Iguanas are bright green with a crest of spines from their necks to their striped tails.
• An iguana's tail makes up two-thirds of its length.
• Iguanas eat insects and vegetation. (Instead of porridge, the iguanas could have bowls of vegetables.)
Look at the **Nonfiction Resource** section for books on iguanas.

Goldilocks and the Three Iguanas

Lizards

Let's Create: Good Luck Dragons

Komodo dragons are large meat-eating lizards that live on Komodo Island. This is a small Indonesian island. It is part of a group of islands forming a barrier between the Pacific and Indian oceans.

What You Need:
Komodo Dragon (p. 29), globe, heavy paper, crayons or markers, glitter mixed with glue and stored in squeeze bottles

What You Do:
1. Duplicate a copy of the Komodo Dragon for each child onto heavy paper.
2. Tell the children that some lizards are Komodo dragons. They can grow to be 11 feet (3.6 m) long and can live 50 years. Show the children the Indonesian islands on the globe.
3. Explain that in Chinese legends the dragon is believed to bring good luck. Although the Komodo dragon looks sort of scary, tell the children that they will be making one to hang on their doors for good luck.
4. Give each child a copy of the Komodo dragon.
5. Provide crayons, markers, and glitter mixed with glue for the children to use to decorate their Komodo dragons.
6. Let the children take their Komodo dragons home to post in their rooms for good luck.

Option:
• Have the children share any good luck charms they have.

Komodo Dragon

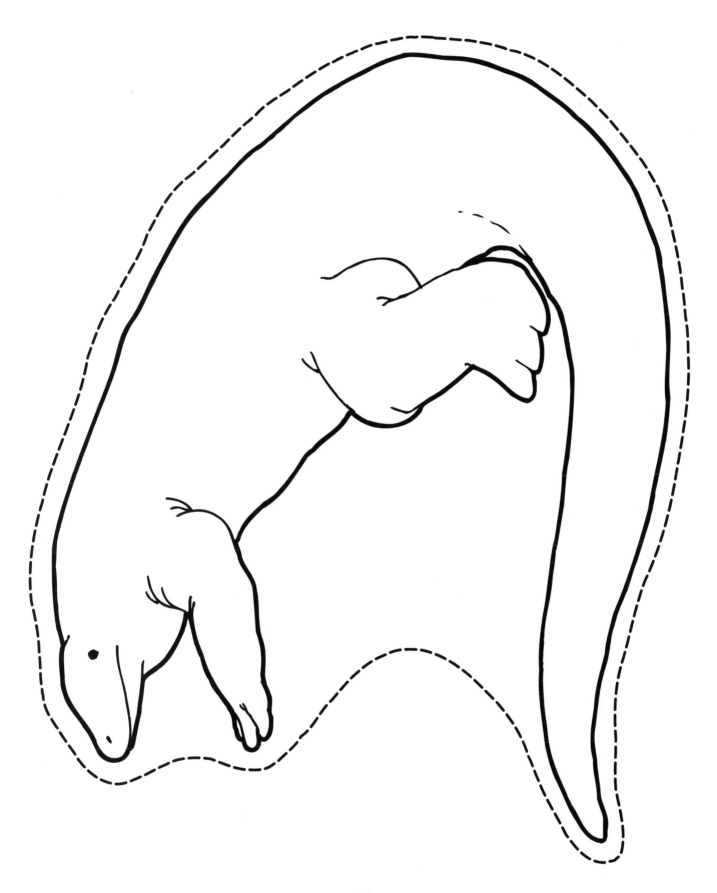

Lizards

Let's Find Out: Chameleon Tongues

A chameleon's tongue can extend farther than the length of its head and body together! A chameleon's tongue extends very quickly. This helps it catch even fast-moving insects or animals.

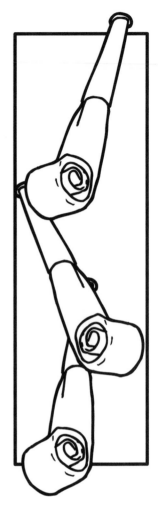

What You Need:
Party blowers (found at party favor stores; one per child), masking tape, permanent marker

What You Do:
1. Explain to the children that a chameleon uses its quick-acting tongue to catch food. Because chameleons move slowly, they need quick tongues to catch their meals.
2. Tell the children the rules of the day. They each will be given a party blower, but they must not aim the blowers at each other. Also, they should never exchange their blowers.
3. Write each child's name on a piece of masking tape. Use this to label each child's blower.
4. Give each child his or her own personal party blower. Let the children pretend to be chameleons catching prey. They can extend their party blower "tongues" as quickly as possible! Tell the children that even when chameleons catch a snack, they start to hunt again immediately. Chameleons in the wild are always hungry! Children should take their blowers home after using them.

Lizards

Let's Find Out: Clip-on Chameleons

Chameleons are found in trees. They grip onto the branches tightly. However, when they're scared, they let go of their grip and fall to the ground. Even baby lizards do this! Most of their enemies will not follow them.

What You Need:
Clothespins, colored felt, glue, wiggly eyes, cardboard, scissors

What You Do:
1. Give each child a clothespin. Explain that they will be turning their clothespins into little chameleons.
2. Have the children glue scraps of colored felt to their clothespins. The children can make many-colored chameleons or make chameleons that are all one color. (If they're making baby chameleons, they should use gray or brown. These colors help the babies blend in with bark or dirt.)
3. Provide wiggly eyes for the children to glue to the front of their chameleons.
4. Cut a strip of cardboard for each child. The children can pretend the cardboard strips are branches. They can clip their chameleons to the branches.

Options:
• Make one large branch for all of the little chameleons to cling to.
• Label each child's chameleon with his or her name.
• Children can clip their chameleons to their coat collars.

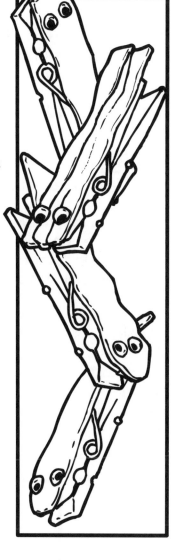

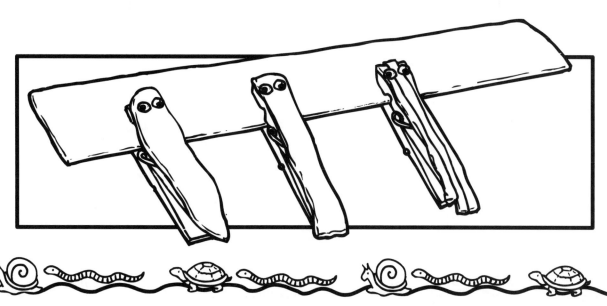

Lizards

Let's Find Out: How Lizards Shed

Lizards shed throughout their lives. However, they do the most growing (and shedding) during their first year.

What You Need:
Clip-on Chameleons (p. 31), old nylons (or Peds), scissors

What You Do:
1. Cut the feet from the old nylons. Give each child one foot or one Ped.
2. Explain to the children that as chameleons grow, they shed their skin. The outer layer of skin flakes off. It leaves a new, brighter skin in its place.
3. Have the children put their clip-on chameleons in the nylon feet.
4. The children can pretend that their chameleons are getting bigger. Then they can pull their clip-on chameleons out of the nylons, shedding the old skin!

Option:
• The children can store their chameleons in the nylon feet for safe keeping.

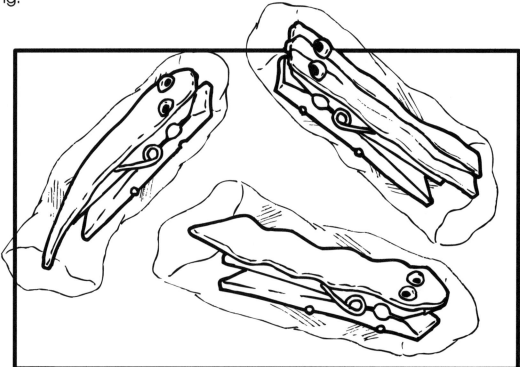

Lizards

Let's Play: Cool Chameleon Color Match

What You Need:
Cool Chameleons (p. 34), crayons (red, orange, yellow, green, blue, purple, black, brown), laminating machine or contact paper

What You Do:
1. Duplicate the Cool Chameleon cards twice.
2. Color the cards to match the words, leaving the white card blank. (Make sure you have two cards of each color.)
3. Cut the cards apart, laminate them, and cut them out again, leaving a thin laminate border to prevent peeling.
4. Explain the game to the children. Turn the cards face down. Each child turns over two cards at a time. If the cards match, the child names the color and keeps the cards. He or she then takes another turn. If the cards do not match, the child turns the cards back over and another child takes a turn.

Option:
• Make a set for each child. The children can color their own cards, cut them apart, and keep them in a resealable bag for storage. They can take the sets home to practice color words with their families.

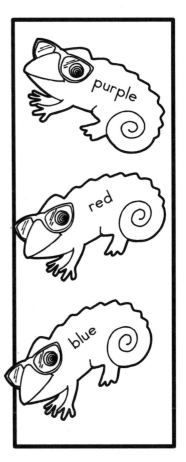

Cool Chameleons

yellow

green

purple

black

blue

orange

brown

red

white

Lizards

Let's Eat: Iguana Food

Although some iguanas eat insects and small rodents, most iguanas eat fruits, vegetables, and leaves.

What You Need:

A variety of fresh fruits (apples, oranges, strawberries, and so on), knife (for adult use only), large bowl, large spoon, small bowls, small plates, plastic forks or spoons, napkins

What You Do:

1. Explain the iguana diet to the children. Then tell them that they will be trying some of the foods that iguanas like to eat.
2. Ahead of time, cut the fruit into small pieces. Keep the types of fruit in separate bowls.
3. Let the children help mix the fruit salad by adding the fruits in separate bowls to the main bowl.
4. Serve the fruit salad and let the children enjoy this healthy snack!

Option:

• Serve cut up vegetables for the children to eat. (Add dip, for extra flavor.)

Lizards

Let's Sing: Do You Have Green Skin?
To the tune of "Do Your Ears Hang Low?"

Do you have green skin?
Can you shed the skin you're in?
Can you change the color, too?
Turn from green to red to blue?
Do you live up in the trees,
Blending in with sticks and leaves?
Do you have green skin?

Let's Sing: I'm a Lizard
(to the tune of "Alouette")

I'm a lizard,
Yes, I am a lizard,
I'm a lizard,
I can shed my skin.
When it's time to shed my skin,
I can shed the skin I'm in.
Shed my skin,
Shed my skin.
Skin I'm in,
Skin I'm in.
Ohhhh,
I'm a lizard,
Yes, I am a lizard,
I'm a lizard,
I can shed my skin.

"I'm a Lizard!"

Turtles

Introduction

• Let's Read:
Yertle the Turtle by Dr. Seuss (Random House, 1950).
Yertle the Turtle is king of the turtles. In order to view his entire kingdom, he climbs on top of his turtle subjects. Not satisfied, he demands that more and more turtles join the stack...until it collapses! After that, all turtles are free to do what they want.

• Let's Talk:
Ask if the children have ever wanted to be king or queen. What would it mean to them to have a kingdom? Would they want a castle and servants? Would they expect other people to do what they told them to? Let the children share their visions of what it might be like to be king or queen. Then ask if they think it is better for everyone to be equal—like the turtles at the end of the story.

• Let's Learn:
There are between 250 and 300 types of turtles. Their shells protect them from the weather and also help them to blend in with their surroundings. A turtle can tuck its legs and head into its shell for protection. It does this when it is frightened. Some turtles live in the ocean and only go on shore to lay their eggs. These turtles use their flippers like boat oars to move through the water. The largest turtle ever found was a leatherback that weighed 2,016 pounds (752 kg)!

Turtles

Let's Create: Stacking Turtles

After reading *Yertle the Turtle*, the children can play their own turtle stacking game.

What You Need:
Margarine tubs with lids (one per child), colored stickers, white circle stickers, markers

What You Do:
1. Give each child an empty margarine tub.
2. Explain that the children will be turning their tubs into turtles. They can decorate the turtle "shells" with colored stickers.
3. Give each child a circular white sticker to use to make the turtle's face. Each child can attach this sticker on the front of his or her turtle.
4. Once the turtles are decorated, play a *Yertle the Turtle* stacking game! Have the children see how many margarine tub turtles they can stack before the tubs tip over.

Options:
• If margarine tubs are not available, children can use cream cheese tubs, cottage cheese containers, yogurt containers, or Tupperware tubs. For the stacking game, it helps if all tubs are about the same size.

Let's Create: A Fable Book

What You Need:
A version of "The Tortoise and the Hare," paper, crayons or markers, hole punch, brads

What You Do:
1. Tell the children the fable about the tortoise and the hare. If you do not know it by heart, refer to the book links below.
2. Stage a race in which one child plays at being the tortoise and the other pretends to be the hare. Give each child a chance to play at least one part!
3. Have the children decide which creature they would rather be—the tortoise or the hare. Let the children explain their reasons for their choices. Then have the children guess the moral—or lesson—of the story.
4. Let the children draw pictures of the race. Have each child dictate a sentence or two about his or her picture. Bind the pictures together in a class version of "The Tortoise and the Hare."

Option:
• Act out other fables from Aesop. Let the children guess the moral each time.

Note:
The name "tortoise" refers to turtles that live on land.

Turtles

Let's Create: Paper Plate Turtles

Different turtles have different types of shells. Before doing this activity, show the children color photographs of different kinds of turtles for inspiration. Of course, the children's own versions of turtles do not have to be realistic!

What You Need:

Paper plates (one per child), tempera paint, shallow tins for paint, sponges (cut into different shapes), newsprint, construction paper, scissors, glue

What You Do:

1. Cover the workstation with newsprint.
2. Explain that each child will be making his or her own turtle.
3. Give each child a paper plate.
4. Demonstrate how to use the sponge pieces to print designs on the backs of the paper plates.
5. Once the children have finished printing their turtles, let the turtles dry.
6. While the turtles dry, the children can cut out four feet and a head for their turtles.
7. The children can glue the head and feet to the dry turtles.
8. Set the turtles around the room for display. Put them on tables near books about turtles.

Options:

• For variety, provide different sizes of plates. The children can choose whether they want to make adult turtles or baby turtles.
• Use paper bowls instead of paper plates. The activity is the same, with the children gluing on heads and feet after the bowls dry.

41

Turtles

Let's Create: Colorful Turtles

What You Need:
Fingerpaint, shallow tins (for paint), fingerpaint paper, scissors, construction paper, glue, newsprint

What You Do:
1. Cover the workstation with newsprint.
2. Cut the fingerpaint paper into circles.
3. Give each child a circle of paper. Have the children fold their papers in half and then open them up again.
4. Show the children how to paint on only one half of their circles. Once they're finished, demonstrate how to fold the papers in half and seal them together.
5. When the children open the papers, their artwork will have "magically" appeared on the blank side.
6. Let the papers dry. While they dry, have the children cut out four feet and a head for their turtles.
7. The children can glue the head and limbs onto their dry turtle shells.
8. Post the colorful turtles on a "Terrific Turtles" bulletin board.

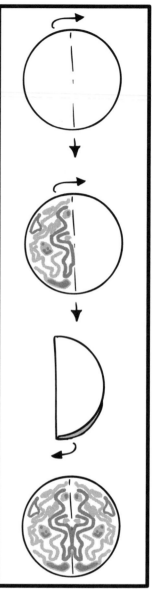

Turtles

Let's Find Out: Digging for Treasures

Sea turtles lay their eggs in holes by the sea. Then they cover up the eggs and go back to the ocean. Environmentalists often dig up the eggs and move them to a safer spot, which gives the eggs a better chance to hatch. They release the baby turtles to the sea.

What You Need:
Ping-Pong balls, sand table or sand box

What You Do:
1. Explain that people who care about animals are trying to help save animals that are in trouble. These animals may be in trouble for a variety of reasons, such as changes in their environment. People who care about sea turtles often dig up their eggs and place them in safe spots to hatch.
2. Bury the Ping-Pong balls in the sand table or sand box.
3. Explain that the children will be digging up the "turtle eggs" in the same way that people who care about sea turtles do.
4. Have groups of children work to uncover the eggs. When they are finished, they should rebury the eggs for the next group of children to find.

Book Link:
• *When Turtles Come to Town* by Cary B. Ziter, photographs by Chuck Bigger (Franklin Watts, 1989). This book illustrates how people work to save the sea turtles. The language may be too difficult for small children, but it's an easy story to paraphrase.

Turtles

Let's Find Out: Turtle Babies

A mama sea turtle lays her eggs in a hole dug in the sand. The eggs are about the size of a Ping-Pong ball. When the eggs hatch, after about 50 days, the little turtles make their way to the sea.

What You Need:
Baby Turtles (p. 45), Stacking Turtles (p. 39), plastic eggs (available at Easter), crayons or markers, scissors

What You Do:
1. Duplicate the Baby Turtles and cut them out. Make enough for each child to have two.
2. Have the children color their Baby Turtles.
3. Give each child two plastic eggs. Have the children put one Baby Turtle into each egg.
4. Show the children how to store the eggs inside their Stacking Turtles.
5. Let the children undo the margarine tub lids and let their turtle eggs out. They can then open the eggs to free the Baby Turtles!
6. The children can take their Stacking Turtles and Baby Turtles to play with at home.

Option:
• If plastic eggs are not available, substitute Ping-Pong balls. However, the Baby Turtles won't fit inside.

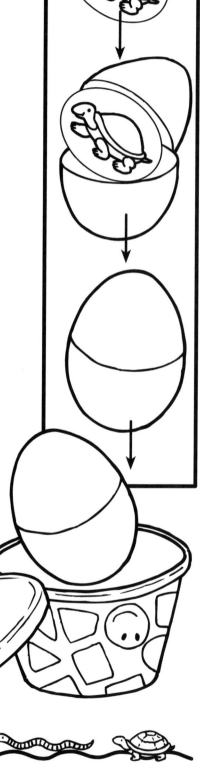

Baby Turtles

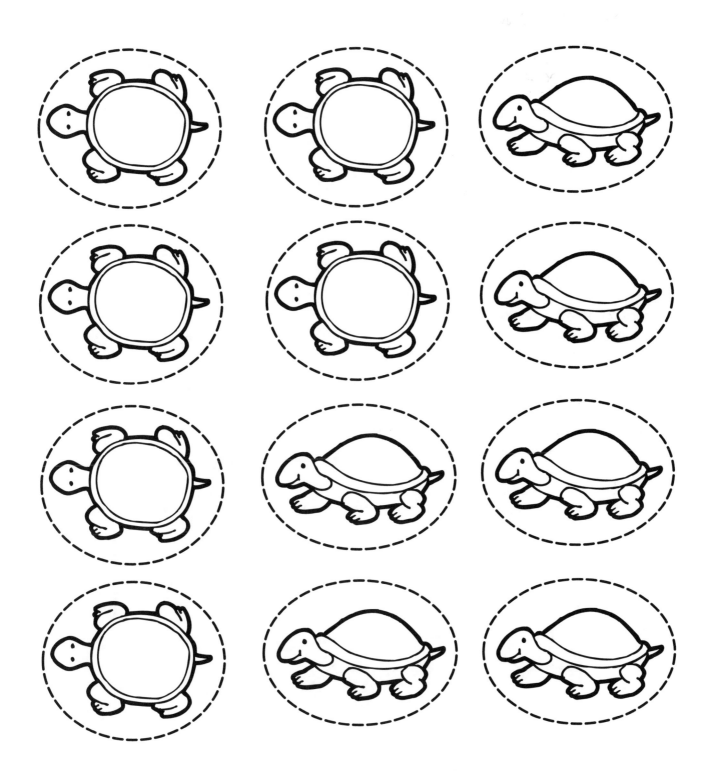

Turtles

Let's Play: Turtle, Turtle, to the Sea

What You Need:
Markers and Spinner (p. 47), Game Board pattern (p. 48), crayons or markers, clear contact paper (or laminating machine), scissors, hole punch, brad

What You Do:
1. Duplicate the Game Board pattern, color, and cover with contact paper. (Or use a laminating machine.)
2. Duplicate the Markers and Spinner, cut out, color, cover with clear contact paper, and cut out again. (Leave a thin laminate border to help prevent peeling.)
3. Punch a hole in the center of the spinner, and attach the arrow using the brad.
4. Explain the game. Three children may play at a time. Each child is a little sea turtle trying to reach the ocean. The first child spins the spinner and moves to the next similarly shaped spot on the board. The first child to land at the spot marked "finish" is the winner.

Markers & Spinner

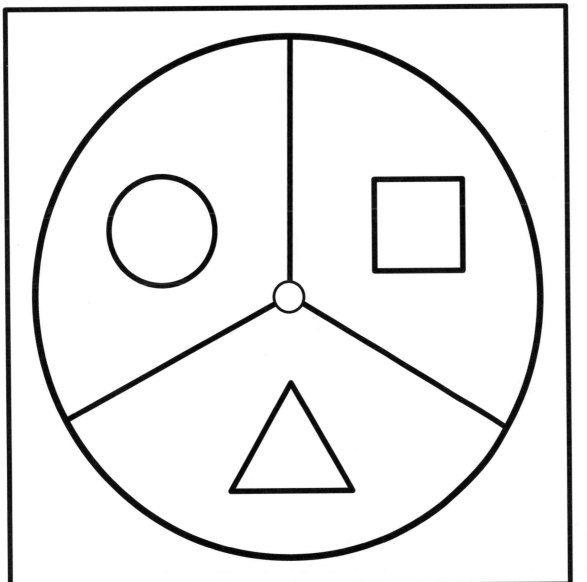

Game Board

FINISH

START

48

Turtles

Let's Sing: I'm a Turtle
(to the tune of "Alouette")

I'm a turtle,
Yes, I am a turtle.
I'm a turtle,
I live in a shell.
When I want to go to sleep,
I pull in my head and feet.
Go to sleep,
Go to sleep,
Head and feet,
Head and feet.
Ohhhh,
I'm a turtle,
Yes, I am a turtle.
I'm a turtle,
I live in a shell.

I'm a Little Turtle
(to the tune of "I'm a Little Teapot")

I'm a little turtle,
On the sand,
I go slow when on dry land.
When I'm in the ocean, watch and see—
I'm so quick you can't catch me!

I'm a turtle,
Yes, I am a turtle.
I'm a turtle,
I live in a shell.

"I'm a Turtle!"

Alligators & Crocodiles

Introduction

• Let's Read:
Lyle, Lyle Crocodile by Bernard Waber (Houghton Mifflin, 1965). Lyle is a loveable crocodile who lives with the Primm family. Everyone loves Lyle except a neighbor named Mr. Grumps and his cat Loretta. However, when Lyle rescues Mr. Grumps and Loretta from an apartment fire, both Mr. Grumps and his cat change their minds about the helpful crocodile. In the same series: *Loveable Lyle*, *Lyle and the Birthday Party*, and *Lyle Finds His Mother*.

• Let's Talk:
This book provides a perfect opportunity to discuss fire safety. Remind the children of the fire procedure of your school. If possible, set up a drill. Consider inviting a fire fighter to speak with the children—or take a field trip to a fire station where children can view a fire truck close up!

• Let's Learn:
Crocodiles and alligators are reptiles. This means that their body temperatures are the same as the air or the water around them. They lie around in the sun to get warm and in the shade to get cool. Crocodiles and alligators belong to the same family of animals, called crocodilians. Crocodilians are the largest reptiles in the world! Crocodiles are faster and more fierce than alligators. Alligators can stay under the water at least an hour holding their breath! Baby alligators and crocodiles hatch from eggs. The mother lays between 30 and 60 eggs at a time.

Note:
Consider taking the children on a field trip to a local zoo or aquarium to see alligators or crocodiles.

Refer to the **Nonfiction Resources** at the end of the book for a list of resources that feature photographs and drawings of alligators and crocodiles.

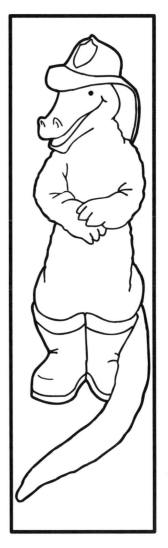

Alligators & Crocodiles

Let's Create: Lovable as Lyle

Lyle is a lovable crocodile. Everyone thinks so. By the end of the book, even Mr. Grumps and Loretta the cat agree!

What You Need:
Lyle, Lyle, Crocodile by Bernard Waber (Houghton Mifflin, 1965), white paper, crayons or markers

What You Do:
1. After reading *Lyle, Lyle, Crocodile*, discuss why people thought Lyle was lovable.
2. Have the children share reasons why they think *they* are lovable.
3. Give each child a sheet of white paper. Have the children illustrate reasons why they are lovable on their papers. Help children brainstorm reasons if they need help. (They might be lovable because they share toys with friends or because they clean up after themselves.)
4. Post the finished pictures on a "We're as Lovable as Lyle" bulletin board.

Alligators & Crocodiles

Let's Find Out: How Crocodiles Brush

Crocodiles in the Nile eat almost anything. However, these crocodiles never eat Egyptian plovers (a type of bird). A Nile crocodile won't eat a plover even if the bird climbs into its mouth. Why? Because the birds pick the crocodile's teeth, keeping its mouth clean!

What You Need:
Plover Patterns (p. 54), file folders (one per child), crayons and markers, scissors

What You Do:
1. Explain the relationship between the plover and the Nile crocodile.
2. Give each child a file folder.
3. Have each child illustrate the inside and outside of the folder to look like a crocodile's mouth. They can draw teeth inside and two eyes on the top.
4. Give each child a plover pattern to color and cut out.
5. Each child can use a plover to pretend to clean the crocodile's mouth.

Option:
• Use this activity to discuss dental health. Remind children to brush after each meal. Invite a dentist in to talk to the children.

Book Link:
• *Bill and Pete Go Down the Nile* by Tomie dePaola (Putnam's, 1987).
Bill is a little crocodile who lives in the Nile. Pete is his friend and his toothbrush!

Plover Patterns

Alligators & Crocodiles

Let's Find Out: Where Alligators Come From

Crocodiles and alligators build different nests, but both types of nests keep the eggs warm. Alligators build nests above the ground. Crocodiles dig holes in the ground and lay the eggs in the holes.

What You Need:
Little 'Gators (p. 56), scissors, crayons or markers, plastic eggs (available at Easter; one per child), basket

What You Do:
1. Duplicate enough Little 'Gators for each child to have one. Cut them out.
2. Give each child a Little 'Gator to color with crayons or markers. Write each child's name on the back of his or her 'gator.
3. Give each child a plastic egg. Have the children put their Little 'Gators in the eggs.
4. Collect the eggs and put them in a basket.
5. Have the children sit in a circle. One at a time, let the children choose an egg and open it up. Help the children to read the name on the back of the Little 'Gator. Have the children reunite the 'gators with their owners.
6. Let the children take home their eggs and 'gators.

Note:
This is a good name-recognition activity. Or use it at the start of the year to help children get to know each other!

Little 'Gators

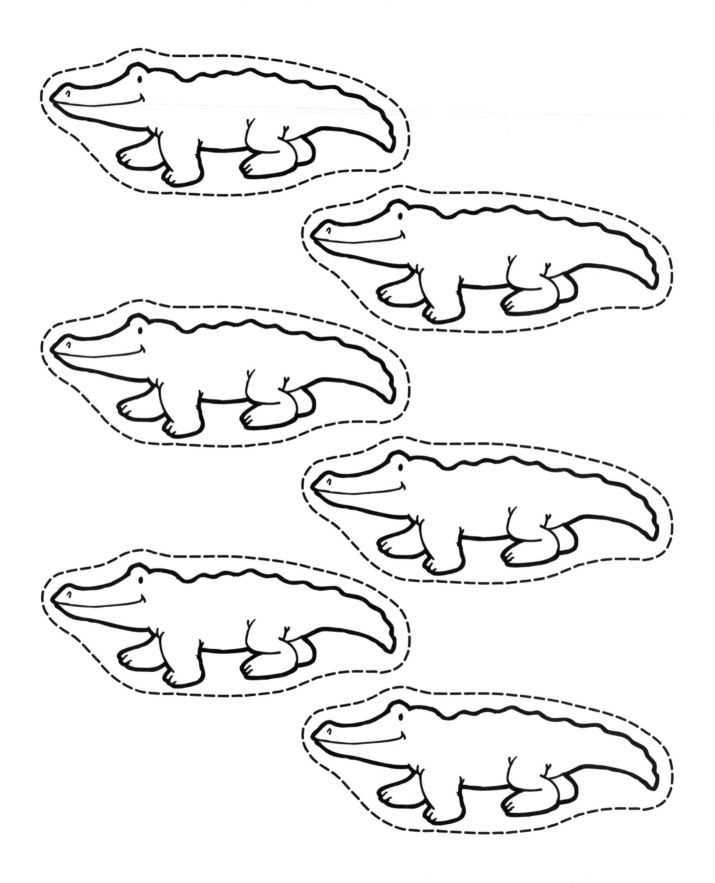

Alligators & Crocodiles

Let's Play: Along the Nile

What You Need:
Markers and Spinner (p. 58), Game Board pattern (p. 59), crayons or markers, clear contact paper (or laminating machine), scissors, hole punch, brad

What You Do:
1. Duplicate the Game Board pattern, color, and cover with contact paper. (Or use a laminating machine.)
2. Duplicate the Markers and Spinner, cut out, color, cover with clear contact paper, and cut out again. (Leave a thin laminate border to help prevent peeling.)
3. Punch a hole in the center of the spinner, and attach the arrow using the brad.
4. Explain the game. Three childen may play at a time. The children travel along the Nile, stepping on the backs of crocodiles. The first child spins the spinner and moves to the next similarly shaped spot on the board. The first child to land at the spot marked "finish" is the winner.

Let's Play: Crocodile Tag
Lyle likes to skip rope, ice skate, and play tag. Play a game of tag in which the child who is "it" is called "Lyle."

Markers & Spinner

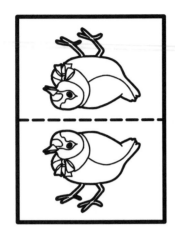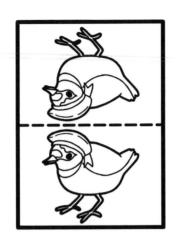

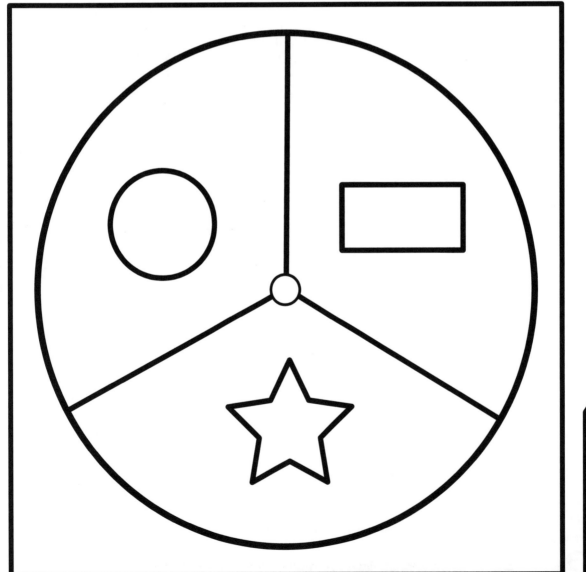

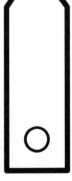

Game Board Pattern

FINISH

START

Alligators & Crocodiles

Let's Eat: Crocodile Snacks

What You Need:
Canned tuna, mayonnaise, seasonings (salt, pepper, paprika, etc.), dill relish (optional), crackers, paper plates, napkins, large bowl and spoon

What You Do:
1. Explain that crocodiles will eat almost anything that comes near the water. They don't normally eat large animals, but prefer creatures like small antelope. Mostly, crocodiles and alligators eat fish.
2. Add the desired amount of mayonnaise and seasonings to the tuna.
3. Let the children help stir the salad.
4. Serve tuna salad on crackers to your hungry little crocodilians!

Note:
Be sure to check with parents for food allergies before serving this, or any snack, to the children.

Option:
• Serve goldfish crackers instead of tuna salad.

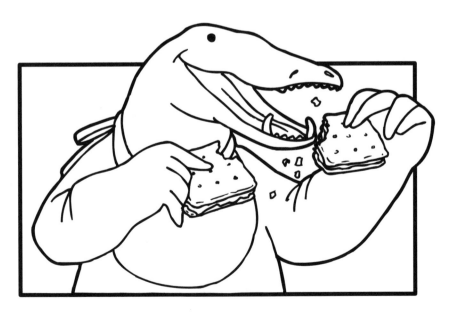

Alligators & Crocodiles

Let's Sing: Do You Like to Smile?
(to the tune of "Do Your Ears Hang Low?")

Do you like to smile
Like a hungry crocodile?
Are you sort of like a 'gator,
Since you both are called reptiles?
When you close your mouth to grin,
Are your teeth outside or in?
Do you like to smile?

Note: When alligators close their mouths, only their top teeth are visible. Even when crocodiles close their mouths, almost all of their teeth can be seen.

Let's Sing: I'm a 'Gator
(to the tune of "Alouette")

I'm a 'gator,
I'm an alligator,
I'm a 'gator,
You can check my smile.
When I close my mouth up tight,
Only my top teeth shine bright.
Mouth up tight.
Mouth up tight.
Teeth shine bright,
Teeth shine bright.
Ohhhh,
I'm a 'gator,
I'm an alligator.
I'm a 'gator,
You can check my smile.

Let's Learn: A Fun Reptile Rhyme
See you later, alligator.
After awhile, crocodile.

"I'm an Alligator!"

"I'm a Crocodile!"

Snails & Slugs

Introduction

• Let's Read:
The Snail's Spell by Joanne Ryder, illustrated by Lynne Cherry (Viking, 1992). A Children's Science Book Award Winner. This fanciful story takes children on an imaginary journey. Readers become snails, visualizing what it would be like to live in a snail's shell, to travel through the garden observing the surrounding world. Beautiful illustrations accompany the soothing text.

• Let's Talk:
Have the children try to imagine what it would be like to be a snail. Would it be scary? Would they enjoy being so small? Have the children share the positive and negative aspects of being a snail. Children can also share other animals they might like to be—or at least pretend to be!

• Let's Learn About Snails:
Snails are not reptiles. They are a type of animal called a mollusk. Other mollusks include clams, oysters, octopuses, and squid. Snails have two long feelers on the tops of their heads. The feelers look a little bit like horns. The snail's eyes are on the tip of the feelers. Snails have no bones. A snail lives in its shell. The shell grows as it grows. When a snail is scared or tired, it tucks in its feelers and then draws its head and body into its shell. A snail's shell goes everywhere the snail goes! Some snails live on land. Most live in water.

• Let's Learn About Slugs:
Snails without shells are called slugs. Some slugs live on land. Others live in the sea. Sea slugs come in different colors. This helps sea slugs to blend in with their surroundings. By blending in, sea slugs avoid their enemies.

Note:
Many natural history museums have collections of snail shells. Consider taking the children on a field trip to see shells of land and marine snails.

Snails & Slugs

Let's Create: A Snail's View Mural

Read *The Snail's Spell* before starting this activity.

What You Need:
Butcher paper, crayons, markers, tempera paint, paintbrushes, tins for paint

What You Do:
1. Have the children imagine that they are snails. Read them *A Snail's Spell*, or take them on your own imaginary trip— having them imagine that they are small creatures who live in a garden.
2. Explain to the children that they will be making a mural. They will work together to paint a picture of what a garden might look like from a snail's point of view.
3. Have the children discuss what they would like to put on the picture. You can help them by writing down the items they suggest on a chalkboard.
4. Divide the children into groups. Each group should work on the mural for a designated time.
5. Spread a large sheet of butcher paper on a flat surface. Provide crayons, markers, paints, paintbrushes, and other supplies for the children to use to create their mural.
6. When the mural is finished, post it on a wall in the room. Label it "A Snail's View."

Snails & Slugs

Let's Create: Snail Trail Pictures

What You Need:
Fingerpaint paper, fingerpaint, shallow tins for paint, colored construction paper, scissors, glue

What You Do:
1. Cut out snail shapes from the colored construction paper. (You can use the snail on this page as a template.)
2. Explain to the children that when snails travel, they leave a trail behind. If possible, show children a snail trail on a sidewalk outside.
3. Provide fingerpaint paper and fingerpaint. Have the children dip one finger at a time in the paint and make swirling trails along the papers.
4. Give each child one or several snails to glue to the snail trail pictures after the paint has dried.
5. Post the pictures on a "Snail Trail" bulletin board.

Option:
• Mix glitter into the fingerpaint to make shimmering pictures.

Snails & Slugs

Let's Create: Snail Lace

In *The Lace Snail* by Betsy Byars, a small snail is suddenly able to make trails of lace. Many different animals want her lace, from the bugs who want parachutes to the crocodile who wants a hammock. The snail makes something for everyone before her lace runs out.

What You Need:
Colored construction paper, bits of lace, glue, crayons or markers, scissors, non-toxic ink pads

What You Do:
1. Give each child a sheet of colored construction paper.
2. Using the ink pads, show the children how to make thumbprints on their papers. The thumbprints will become snail shells.
3. Have the children use crayons or markers to draw antenna on their snails.
4. Provide bits of lace for children to glue in trails behind their snails.
5. Post the snail lace pictures on a bulletin board in the classroom.

Book Link:
• *The Lace Snail* by Betsy Byars (Viking, 1975). Children can recreate the pictures in this book by drawing different animals and adding lace the way the snail did.

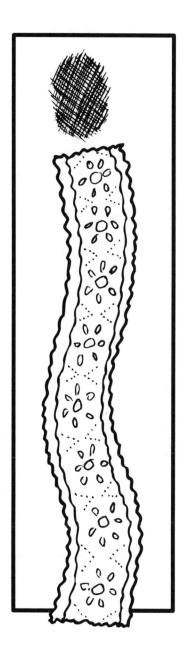

Snails & Slugs

Let's Create: Houses for Snails

What You Need:
Walnut shells (one half per child), scraps of colored felt, glue, marbles (one per child), pipe cleaners (cut into short pieces), scissors

What You Do:
1. Explain to the children that snails are little animals that carry their "house" on their backs.
2. Explain that the children will be designing their own houses for snails.
3. Give each child a half of a walnut shell.
4. Provide scraps of colored felt for the children to glue to the shells.
5. Show the children how to glue two short pieces of pipe cleaner to the front of the shells.
6. When the shells have dried, give each child a marble. They can sit the shell on top of the marble and then roll their snails on any flat surface.

Options:
• The children can glue a wiggly eye to each pipe cleaner feeler.
• Instead of walnut shells, children can fashion snail shells from playdough.

Snails & Slugs

Let's Find Out: Other Words for "Snails"

What You Need:
Pictures of snails, drawing paper, crayons or markers

What You Do:
1. Explain to the children that in other parts of the world, people have different words for "snail." In France, snails are called "escargot" (es-car-go). In Italy, snails are called "maruzze." In Germany, snails are "Schnecken." In Spain, a snail is known as a "caracol" (ca-ra-col). Have the children practice saying these different words.
2. Show the children pictures of snails. Have them brainstorm words that describe snails.
3. Give each child a piece of paper.
4. Have the children draw pictures of snails.
5. Let each child have a turn dictating a word or a descriptive phrase for his or her snail.
6. Post the finished pictures on a bulletin board that lists the different foreign words for snails.

Note:
If any of the children in your class speak other languages, have them share their country's word for snail.

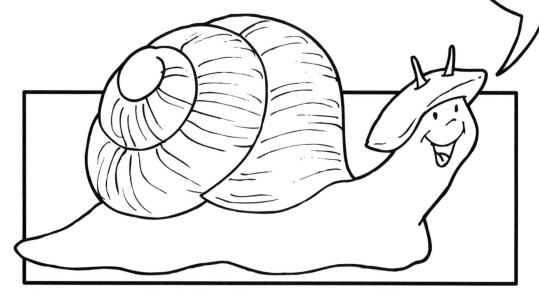

Snails & Slugs

Let's Find Out: "S" Words

In the story *Some Smug Slug*, almost every word starts with the letter "s."

What You Need:
Some Smug Slug by Pamela Duncan Edwards, illustrated by Henry Cole (HarperCollins, 1996), paper, crayons or markers, hole punch, brads

What You Do:
1. Read the book *Some Smug Slug* to the children.
2. Have the children listen for all the "s" sounds in the book.
3. After you've finished reading the book, have the children share as many different "s" words as they can.
4. Give each child a sheet of paper.
5. Have each child choose a word that starts with "s" to illustrate.
6. When the pictures are finished, bind them in a "Super Special 'S'" book.

Options:
• Give each child a small ball of playdough. Have the children make slugs from the playdough. Then show the children how to fashion "s" shapes from their slugs.
• Throughout the year, make alliteration books for all the letters in the alphabet.

Supper starts with 's.'

Snails & Slugs

Let's Play: Super Snail Trail

What You Need:
Markers and Spinner (p. 72), Game Board pattern (p. 73), crayons or markers, clear contact paper (or laminating machine), scissors, hole punch, brad

What You Do:
1. Duplicate the Game Board pattern, color, and cover with contact paper. (Or use a laminating machine.)
2. Duplicate the Markers and Spinner, cut out, color, cover with clear contact paper, and cut out again. (Leave a thin laminate border to help prevent peeling.)
3. Punch a hole in the center of the spinner, and attach the arrow using the brad.
4. Explain the game. Three children may play at a time. The children travel around the trail of the giant snail until they reach its center. The first child spins the spinner and moves to the next similarly shaped spot on the board. The first child to land at the spot marked "end" is the winner.

Markers & Spinner

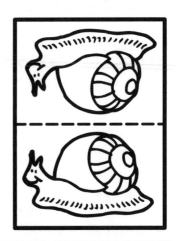

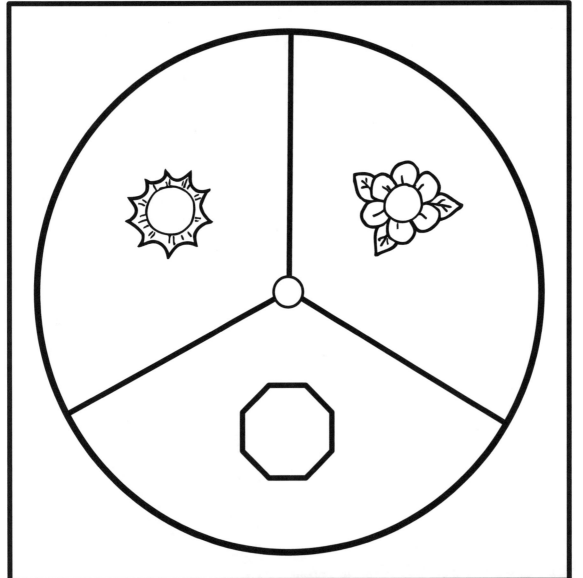

Game Board Pattern

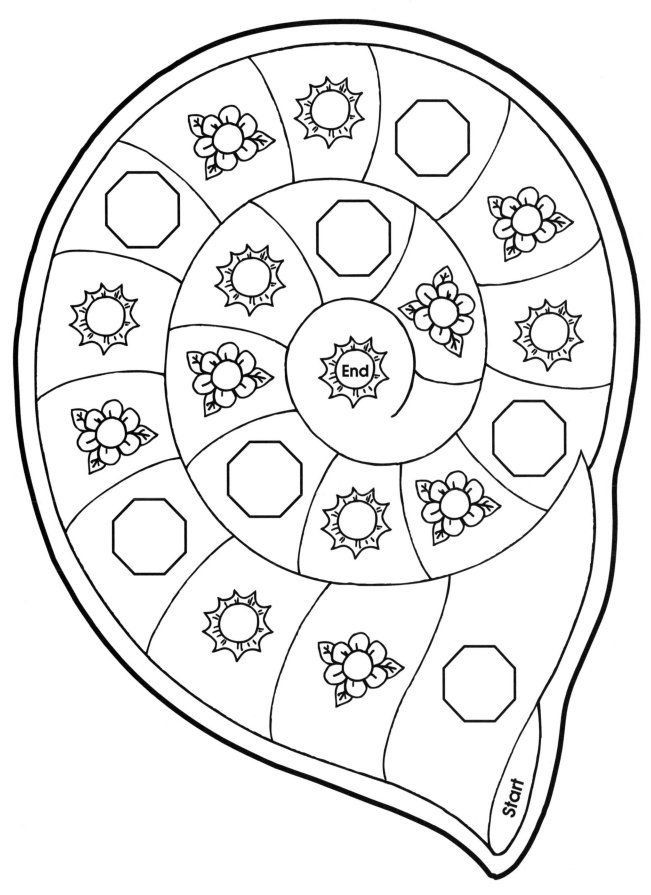

Snails & Slugs

Let's Eat: Stupendous Snail Snacks

Common garden snails eat many kinds of plant leaves. A snail's teeth are on its tongue. It chews by sticking out its tongue and scraping bits of lettuce into its mouth. Even children who don't like salad may like eating it while pretending to be snails!

What You Need:
Salad ingredients (including different types of lettuces), dressing, large bowl and spoon, paper plates, plastic forks, paper napkins

What You Do:
1. Describe how snails eat. Then explain that snails that live on land eat assorted lettuces and other garden plants and vegetables.
2. Let the children help you make a salad. (Do the washing and chopping ahead of time, and let the children add the individual ingredients.)
3. Toss the salad and serve on paper plates.
4. Let the children sample the super snail snack!

Snails & Slugs

Let's Sing: I'm a Sea Snail
(to the tune of "Alouette")

I'm a sea snail,
Yes, I am a sea snail,
I'm a sea snail
I live in the sea.
I live in a coral zone,
In my shell, I'm all alone.
Coral zone,
Coral zone,
All alone,
All alone.
Ohhhhh.
I'm a sea snail,
Yes, I am a sea snail,
I'm a sea snail.
I live in the sea.

Note:
Sea snails live in the shallow coral zones
of tropical seas, as well as in tide pools in coastal regions.

Let's Learn: A Mother Goose Snail Rhyme

Snail, snail
Put out your horns,
I'll give you bread
And barley corns.

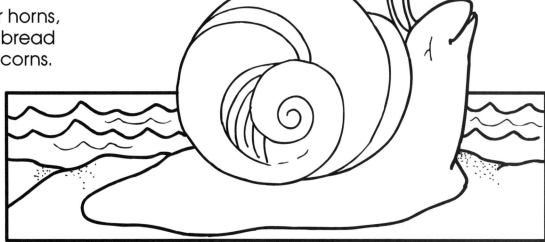

"I'm a Snail!"

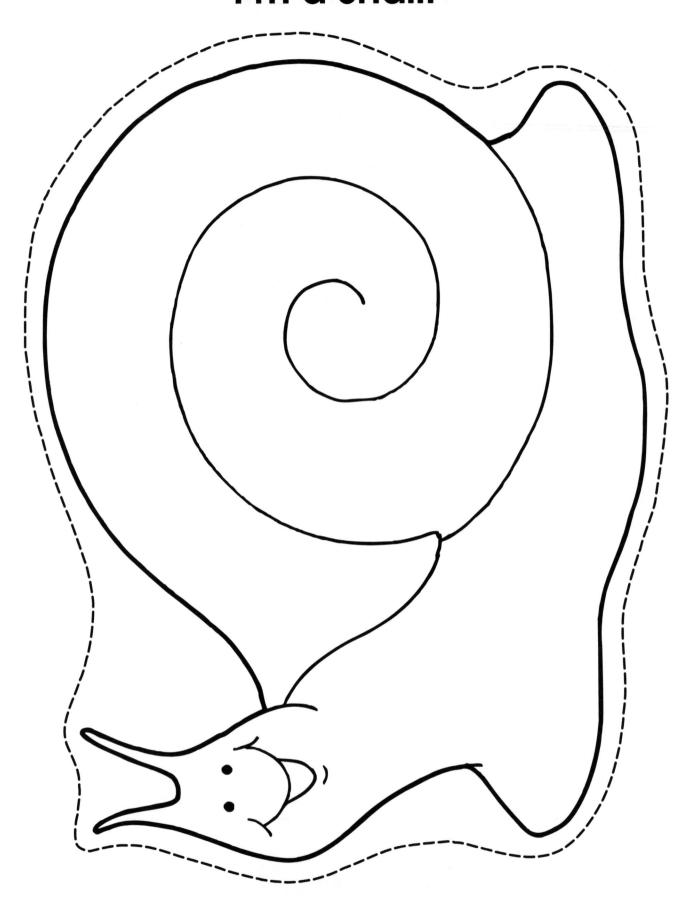

"I'm a Slug!"

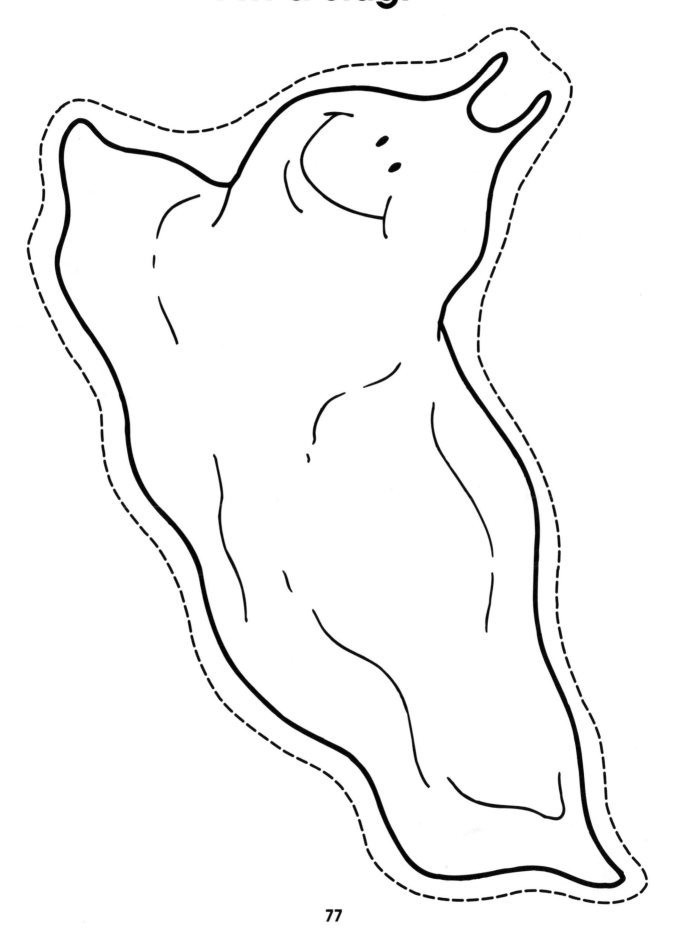

Storybook Resources

Alligators & Crocodiles:
• *Bill and Pete Go Down the Nile* by Tomie dePaola
(Putnam's, 1987).
Bill is a little crocodile who lives in the Nile. On a field trip to a
museum, Bill and his friend Pete save the Sacred Eye of Isis.
• *Cornelius* by Leo Lionni (Knopf, 1983).
In this fable by Lionni, little Cornelius walks upright instead of on
all fours. The other crocodiles aren't impressed. But when
Cornelius learns to stand on his head, the other crocodiles want
to learn how, too.
• *The Importance of Crocus* by Roger Duvoisin (Knopf, 1980).
All of the animals on the farm have special skills except for
Crocus the crocodile. Luckily, by the end of the story, Crocus
discovers his own skill.
• *There's an Alligator Under My Bed* by Mercer Mayer
(Dial, 1987).
A boy solves the problem of the alligator under his bed.

Lizards:
• *The Mixed-Up Chameleon* by Eric Carle (HarperCollins, 1975).
A chameleon wishes it were a little bit like all the different
animals in the zoo. Then it learns that it's best to be just like
himself, after all.
• *They Thought They Saw Him* by Craig Kee Strete, illustrated by
Jose Aruego and Ariane Dewey (Greenwillow, 1996).
Different animals want to catch the little chameleon.

Snails:
• *Hooray for Snail!* by John Stadler (Thomas Y. Crowell, 1984).
• *Snail Saves the Day* by John Stadler (Harper & Row, 1985).

Snakes:
• *The Day Jimmy's Boa Ate the Wash* by Trinka Hakes Noble,
illustrated by Steven Kellogg (Dial, 1980).
• *Jimmy's Boa and the Big Splash Birthday Bash* by Trinka Hakes
Noble, illustrated by Steven Kellogg (Dial, 1989).

Turtles:
• *Franklin Is Bossy* by Paulette Bourgeois (Scholastic, 1993).
Nobody will play with Franklin, a turtle, because he is too bossy.
• *Tracks in the Sand* by Loreen Leedy (Doubleday, 1993).
This beautiful book illustrates the habits of sea turtles.

Nonfiction Resources

Alligators & Crocodiles:
• *Alligator* by Jack Denton Scott (Putnam's, 1984).
Black-and-white photographs are perfect to share with the children.
However, the text is not age-appropriate.
• *Alligators & Crocodiles* by John Bonnett Wexo (Creative Education, 1989).
This mix of four-color illustrations and color photographs will interest children.

Lizards:
• *Chameleons: Dragons in the Trees* by James Martin (Crown, 1991).
This book features beautiful color photographs of a wide variety of chameleons.
• *Iguanas* by W. P. Mara (Capstone, 1996).
This book includes photos and facts. Especially amazing is the picture of the iguanas basking in the sun!
• *Komodo Dragon on Location* by Kathy Darling, photographs by Tara Darling (Lothrop, Lee & Shepard, 1997).
This book contains excellent photographs to share with the children. However, you may wish to avoid the ones of the dragons feeding.

Reptiles:
• *Reptiles* by Colin McCarthy (Knopf, 1991).
This book is filled with interesting facts and four-color photos.
• *What Is a Reptile?* by Robert Snedden (Sierra Club Books for Children, 1994).
Great photos and facts to share.

Snails:
• *Life of the Snail* by Theres Buholzer (Carolrhoda, 1984).
This book is filled with color photographs to show the children. The text is too difficult to read aloud.

Snakes:
• *Amazing Snakes* by Alexandra Parsons (Knopf, 1990).
Children will enjoy looking at the different pictures in this book. The information is interesting to share.
• *A Gathering of Garter Snakes* by Bianca Lavies (Dutton, 1993).
Written and photographed by a true snake lover, this lovely book is filled with amazing photos!

Nonfiction Resources

Snakes (continued):
• *Rattlesnakes* by Russell Freedman (Holiday House, 1984).
Black-and-white photographs are perfect to share.
• *Snakes* by Seymour Simon (HarperCollins, 1992).
The information in this book is for older children, but the large,
color photographs are ideal to share with a class.

Turtles:
• *Turtle Watch* by George Ancona (Macmillan, 1987).
This book about sea turtles is filled with black-and-white
photographs.

Web Sites:

Alligator site:
• http//www.birminghamzoo.com/animals/gator.html

Snail site:
Kiddy House
This web site includes features for children, teachers, and
parents. The snail feature is award-winning.
• http//www.kiddyhouse.com/Snails/

Snake site:
Bayou Bob's Brazos River Rattlesnake Ranch
This site features many snake exhibits, not only
rattlesnakes.
• http//www.wf.net/~snake/index.html

Reptile site:
Honolulu Zoo
This site features tortoises, Nile crocodiles,
lizards, and more. Choose the "zoo tour"
to find the reptile sections.
• http//www.honoluluzoo.org/